Restaurant Employee Retention Strategies

Philip S. Becker

Abstract

Employee retention is a persistent challenge in the restaurant industry.

Business owners are particularly concerned because frequent staff departures

can disrupt operations, increase training costs, and ultimately threaten

business profitability. Grounded in Herzberg's two-factor theory, the purpose

of this qualitative pragmatic inquiry study was to identify restaurant owners'

effective retention strategies in Birmingham, AL. Data sources included

semistructured interviews, public data such as disseminated reports and

websites, Book, including books, and peer-reviewed articles. Thematic

analysis of the data resulted in four themes: (a) compensation, (b)

acknowledgment and rewards, (c) management practices, and (d) a positive

working environment. A key recommendation is to integrate Herzberg's

framework into existing employee engagement models to evaluate their

current HR strategies and mitigate employee retention. The implications for

positive social change include the potential for restaurant and business

owners to reduce unemployment rates, increase profitability, and implement

effective retention strategies.

Table of Contents

Section 1: Foundation of the Project

Background of the Problem

Retaining employees is critical to the success of a restaurant, as they are valuable assets. Employees can either enhance or damage a restaurant's profitability (Elnaga & Imran, 2013). Employee turnover is a significant challenge facing restaurant owners, and the hospitality sector has relatively high levels of turnover, thus negatively impacting an organization's profitability. Dogru et al. (2023) reported that employee turnover across the hospitality industry has been estimated to be between 10% and 15% and increased by 65% over time. Enamala and Reddy (2022) stated that employee retention is paramount for business stability; however, creating and implementing retention strategies can be challenging for some restaurant owners.

Business Problem Focus and Project Purpose

The specific business problem was that some restaurant owners in Birmingham, AL., lack effective strategies to improve employee retention. Therefore, the purpose of this qualitative pragmatic inquiry was to identify and explore effective strategies that restaurant owners use in Birmingham, AL., to improve employee retention. I employed a purposeful sampling approach commonly used in qualitative research. With this approach, researchers can effectively conduct in-depth interviews by selecting participants who can offer targeted insights related to the research questions (Dahal et al., 2024). The targeted population consisted of six restaurant owners with effective strategies to retain employees in their restaurants for individual interviews and the collection of public documents. Data sources for this project consisted of the following: (a) semistructured interviews; (b) public data, such as publicly disseminated reports and public websites; and (c) Book, such as books, peer-reviewed articles, and research findings about practices that are relevant to the inquirer's topic. The conceptual framework for this project was

Herzberg's (1959) two-factor theory.

Research Question

What effective strategies do restaurant owners in Birmingham, AL., use to retain employees?

Assumptions and Limitations

Assumptions

Assumptions are mental shortcuts that facilitate probability and problem-solving judgments, allowing people to operate more efficiently within their natural world (Clair et al., 2022). Clair et al. (2022) stated that an assumption is an unproven belief that allows people to make decisions without tangible truth. There was one assumption associated with this project. I assumed that the participants would answer the interview questions honestly.

Limitations

Research limitations are the weaknesses of the research, depending on factors that are usually out of the researcher's control (Ross & Bibler, 2019). One significant limitation of this project was the time constraint imposed by Walden University's guidelines for completing research studies. Another limitation was that some restaurant owners may depend on others for management decisions, which could result in a lack of immediate information and insights. Additionally, participants may have chosen to withhold crucial details about their business strategies and practices.

Transition

Section 1 provided an overview of the background of the problem of restaurant owners' challenges with employee retention, the business problem focus and project purpose, the research question, and the assumptions and limitations of this project. In Section 2, I will review professional and academic Book and applications to applied business. Section 3 will include the nature of the project, project ethics, the nature of the project, population, sampling, and participants, data collection activities, interview questions, data organization and analysis techniques, and reliability and validity. In Section 4, I will discuss the findings and the implications for business practice, social change, and further research.

Section 2: The Book Review

A Review of the Professional and Academic Book

The purpose of this qualitative pragmatic inquiry was to identify and explore successful strategies that restaurant owners use in Birmingham, AL., to improve employee retention. The Book review centered around the following research question: What effective strategies do restaurant owners in Birmingham, AL., use to retain employees? I analyzed effective strategies employed by restaurant owners to retain employees. The Book review included the conceptual frameworks of Herzberg's two-factor theory and transformational leadership theory.

The Book review was a key aspect of the project, which focuses on thoroughly investigating and analyzing various theoretical resources related to the project (Perifanis & Kitsios, 2023). This Book review examined how various motivators and hygiene factors, such as a positive work environment, opportunities for career development, work-life balance, talent management, and employee well-being, can enhance employee satisfaction and improve retention rates in the restaurant industry. The focus was on strategies that restaurant owners can implement to foster a more engaged and committed workforce.

Search Methodology

My Book review included sources from seminal books and journals. The keywords used for this review included *employee retention, restaurant owners, Birmingham, AL.,* and *strategies.* I researched content using two databases: ProQuest and ScienceDirect. The organization of the Book review was as follows: (a) one-third is about the theory of my conceptual framework, (b) one-third is about the topical foundation of the business topic, and (c) one-third is about other research studies on the business topic and how it applies to the conceptual framework. My Book review contained 85% of peer-reviewed sources, and 95% were published between 2021 and 2025 or within 5 years of my anticipated 2025 graduation

date.

Conceptual Framework

Herzberg's Two-factor Theory

I selected Herzberg's two-factor theory as my conceptual framework. Frederick Herzberg's two-factor theory, known as Herzberg's motivational theory, was developed in 1959 and explained the factors of motivation and satisfaction in workers. The theory advanced by Herzberg has two categories, namely the hygiene factors and the motivating factors. Compensation, organizational culture, and interpersonal relations are hygiene factors that do not contribute to job satisfaction but, if neglected, can lead to dissatisfaction (Koncar et al., 2022). In contrast, factors such as recognition, achievement, and responsibility are the factors that define motivation and satisfaction at work (Uka & Prendi, 2021).

Herzberg's two-factor theory was most appropriate for my project because it helped identify and understand the participants' effective strategies to determine the right approach to retaining employees in the restaurant sector. Knowledge of hygiene and motivating factors can enable restaurant owners to formulate strategies that meet the employees' and higher-order needs. For instance, an effective remuneration procedure can eliminate dissatisfaction, while organizational support and promotion can increase satisfaction and employee turnover.

According to Herzberg et al. (1959), motivated workers are most likely to be satisfied. Koncar et al. (2022) found that satisfied employees consider leaving their employers but do not follow through. Likewise, Uka and Prendi (2021) noted that the level of satisfaction among employees depends on the environmental and psychological factors that are conducive to happiness and comfort. Thus, the given insights can help restaurant owners develop precise retention strategies to satisfy the employees and improve employee retention.

Herzberg's two-factor theory provides a valuable model for developing, analyzing, and improving employee retention practices in the restaurant sector (Thant & Chang, 2021). Combining hygiene and motivating factors can help restaurant owners design working conditions that positively influence employee attitudes toward their jobs and increase turnover rates (Valk & Yousif, 2023). Consequently, understanding and applying Herzberg's two-factor theory can significantly contribute to restaurants' overall success and sustainability in the competitive hospitality industry.

According to Koncar et al. (2022), motivation and demotivation play a central role in retention and are important organizational factors. To elaborate more on these two concepts, Gordon and Parikh (2021) noted that job satisfaction and dissatisfaction are distinct and are not opposites of each other, as discrete factors impact them. Ganesh and Liu (2022) and Uka and

Prendi (2021) also noted that hygiene factors and motivators are crucial for satisfying employees. Strategies for enhancing employee retention for restaurant owners encompass attention to both hygiene factors and motivation. For instance, paying employees fairly and providing a safe environment (hygiene factors) can help prevent dissatisfaction while providing the employees with growth, recognition, and the ability to achieve (motivators) can help increase satisfaction and retain the employees. It is crucial to strive for this dual approach to establish thorough retention strategies that address the employees' basic psychological needs and engage them with the organization's mission.

My project on employee retention involved using Herzberg's two-factor theory to identify and understand the participants' effective strategies. Restaurant owners can use this framework to raise awareness of employees' lower and higher-order needs, increasing productivity. This theoretical application implies that restaurant owners should identify and include hygiene factors and motivators to increase job satisfaction and decrease employee turnover rates. In conclusion, the framework element derived from Herzberg's two-factor theory was suitable to use as a basis for identifying effective strategies for retaining employees. Thus, this theoretical framework and the resultant related findings from the Book were applied to develop conclusions and provide recommendations concerning enhancing staff retention in the restaurant business.

Transformational Leadership Theory

The second component of my composite framework was the transformational leadership theory (Burns, 1978). Burns (1978) proposed that these leaders can enhance their followers' performance. The transformational leadership model includes four primary components: idealized influence, inspirational motivation, individualized consideration, and intellectual stimulation (Sutanto et al., 2021). Burns stated that a transformational leader enhances the performance levels of their followers. Although Burns originally developed the transformational leadership model, Bass (1978) played a crucial role in conceptualizing the model. According to Ladkin and Patrick (2022), Bass's contribution was pivotal in establishing the operational aspects of the transformational leadership model. The transformational leadership model helps address numerous organizational challenges. Nauman (2022) suggested that a transformational leader can positively influence their followers' perceptions, leading to a shared vision and making this leadership model suitable for team building. Based on Burns's work, Eaton (2024) developed the Bass transformational leadership theory. Eaton noted that individuals are more likely to follow a leader who demonstrates confidence, passion, and the ability to inspire them toward achieving common goals. Adopting and developing an appropriate leadership style, such as the transformational one, is vital for an organization's success (Lasrado & Kassem, 2021). Leaders need to recognize the significance of their role in shaping the attitudes and behaviors of their subordinates when implementing strategies to improve employee retention.

The transformational leader represents the four main elements of the model uniquely, motivating employees to exceed expectations and strengthen their loyalty to the organization (Nyakundi et al., 2021). According to Gabriel et al. (2022), the transformational leadership model is connected to improving employee retention.

Zainab et al. (2022) proposed that a transformational leader can positively alter how employees perceive their roles. The altered viewpoint, influenced by the leader's transformational approach, may aid in improving employee retention. According to Gan and Voon (2021), utilizing the transformational leadership model can enhance employee retention. A transformational leader's influential and positive demeanor can reduce the likelihood of employees leaving an organization (Gan & Voon, 2021). From these perspectives, it becomes clear that the role of a transformational leader goes beyond traditional leadership methods and can substantially catalyze employee motivation, satisfaction, and, ultimately, retention within an organization.

The transformational leadership model is a flexible leadership style that effectively addresses various organizational challenges (Tarker, 2021). Al-Subaie (2021) suggested that this model is essential for comprehending and addressing different issues that impact business operations. Employee turnover is a common phenomenon that can negatively impact business operations (Porter & Rigby, 2021). Utilizing the transformational leadership model could benefit restaurant managers when creating employee retention strategies (Gabriel et al., 2022). Applying this leadership model within the context of the restaurant industry could play a pivotal role in addressing and mitigating the challenges associated with employee turnover, ultimately contributing to the overall success and sustainability of business operations.

Alternative Leadership Theories

Numerous leadership styles can effectively address organizational challenges, with the transformational being the most prevalent (Abbas & Ali, 2023). The transactional style employs external motivators such as rewards and punishments to foster employee engagement (Alijumah, 2023; Guarana & Avolio, 2022). While some argue that a manager may exhibit either a transformational or transactional style when addressing organizational issues, Puni et al. (2021) suggested that a leader's behavior may not be exclusively tied to one style and is contingent on the specific context. Consequently, leaders must comprehend the strengths and limitations of different leadership styles when formulating strategies to improve employee retention.

According to Lasrado and Kassem (2021), the transformational leadership theory can be valuable in effectively examining organizational occurrences. Employee turnover is a significant phenomenon to investigate because of the operational disturbances when businesses lose key staff members (Porter & Rigby, 2021). Restaurant managers could enhance their understanding and devise efficient retention strategies by embracing and applying different elements of the transformational leadership model.

Strategies Leaders Use to Retain Employees

According to Ali and Anwar (2021), employee retention strategies must focus on job satisfaction improvements through addressing both job intrinsic and extrinsic factors. These extrinsic factors include the following.

Providing Competitive Compensation and Benefits

The central factor defining satisfaction in most jobs is that employees are well and fairly compensated and feel appreciated in all ways. Competitive pay, health benefits, and retirement reduce employee turnover (Werner & Balkin, 2021).

Organizations must prioritize fair compensation and appreciation of their employees to foster a positive and productive work environment.

Most employees expect to receive paid time off, an essential part of their overall compensation. To compete effectively in the labor market, small business owners can offer paid leave to attract skilled newcomers and retain their current employees (Gabriel & Veronis, 2023). Paid time off encompasses various types of compensation, such as vacation pay, sick pay, and time off for holidays (Hofmarcher, 2021). Businesses that provide their employees with paid time off often experience increased employee retention (Sainju & Hartwell, 2021).

A key benefit that employees seek in a job is healthcare. Workers who frequently take time off because of illness or health issues typically have lower productivity than their employers expect (Henderson & Smith, 2022). Many small business owners recognize the importance of prioritizing employee health. Businesses can enhance employee well-being and productivity by offering benefits (Lovejoy et al., 2021).

Many small business owners offer retirement plans to their employees as part of their benefits packages. These programs often allow employees to invest a portion of their paycheck into a mutual fund of their choice, and the investments grow tax-free until the employee reaches a certain age. Employers may also match a portion of the employees' investment. However, for employers, the IRS regulations governing these programs can be quite burdensome (Hoffman et al., 2021). Both employers and employees can contribute to this type of retirement plan by purchasing pensions or other insurance-based products (Pan et al., 2024).

Positive Work Environment

Another important strategy can be the development of a positive organizational culture. This strategy entails the process of establishing a workplace environment in which employees are respected and appreciated. Measures such as acknowledging people's efforts and achievements, valuing teamwork, and encouraging communication can raise engagement levels to a great extent (Koncar et al., 2022). Acknowledgment will let employees know that their efforts are valued, and they will likely work harder for the organization.

Supportive and inclusive work environments can boost employee morale and satisfaction. Such environments enhance the work climate by building good relationships between the staff and the management, a safe and healthy work environment, and a culture of respect and tolerance (Ali & Anwar, 2021). A supportive work environment can increase creativity, collaboration, and job satisfaction (Basalamah & As'ad, 2021).

Career Development Opportunities

Developing training programs and clear career paths is key to motivating employee tenure. When employees can quickly identify their growth trajectory within the company, they are more likely to remain loyal to the organization (Uka & Prendi, 2021). Companies must invest in creating professional development pathways that empower employees to see a defined trajectory for their advancement within the organization.

Bilderback (2024) emphasized that businesses can cultivate a developmental process by offering employee training. Workers often view training as a valuable job benefit and a chance for career advancement. According to Urme (2023), training and development initiatives enhance employee loyalty and help retain high-performing staff. When companies provide quality on-the-job training, employee retention and satisfaction improve (Elsafty & Oraby, 2022). Well-trained employees typically show more commitment to their roles and higher job satisfaction, boosting productivity and efficiency (Madavi et al., 2022).

Recognition and Rewards

Recognizing and rewarding employees for their hard work and achievements can boost morale and job satisfaction. Implementing programs that acknowledge employee contributions, such as employee of the month awards or performance bonuses, can foster a sense of appreciation and loyalty (Koncar et al., 2022). Organizations should prioritize employee recognition as it enhances employee engagement and contributes to a more productive and cohesive work culture.

Feedback from coworkers and managers is an essential part of employee recognition. Employees appreciate acknowledgment from various sources, including staff, colleagues, stakeholders, managers, supervisors, and customers (Bregenzer et al., 2022). When a job fosters personal development or provides a sense of purpose, it can lead to a feeling of achievement and fulfillment. As long as the work is meaningful and high quality, it contributes to growth and accomplishment (Wahyùdi, 2022).

Work-Life Balance

Offering flexible working hours, remote work options, and adequate vacation time can promote a healthy work-life balance, reduce burnout, and increase job satisfaction. Employees who can balance their work and personal lives are more likely to remain committed to their jobs (Uka & Prendi, 2021). By acknowledging the importance of employee well-being and actively taking steps to support it, organizations can create a more positive and sustainable work environment for their staff.

An environment that prioritizes diversity, inclusivity, and work-life balance can attract and retain a diverse workforce, making the company more creative and dynamic (Leuhery et al., 2024). Employers who support work-life balance by offering wellness initiatives, family leave, and flexible scheduling demonstrate care for their employees' well-being (Kim et al., 2023). This can enhance loyalty and job satisfaction.

Companies encourage creativity and problem-solving by prioritizing diversity and inclusion (Lubis, 2024). Bringing together various perspectives and ideas creates a more egalitarian workplace (Batt-Rawden & Traavik, 2022). Employees are more likely to stay with a company that values their contributions and makes them feel included (Saks, 2022). By fostering a positive corporate culture, businesses can improve employee happiness, engagement, and retention, ultimately contributing to longevity and profitability (Celestin et al., 2024).

Effective Communication

Ensuring transparent and open communication between management and employees can build trust and address concerns before they escalate. Regular feedback sessions, team meetings, and an open-door policy can help employees feel valued and heard (Gordon & Parikh, 2021). By implementing these strategies, restaurant owners can create a work environment that addresses their employees' needs and expectations, leading to higher retention rates and a more motivated and satisfied workforce.

Ndlovu et al. (2021) emphasize that open and honest communication between management and employees fosters a transparent and trustworthy work environment, significantly enhancing employee commitment and job satisfaction. Some leaders may struggle to maintain consistent recognition and communication practices, potentially undermining the effectiveness of these strategies (Franzosa et al., 2022). Mistry et al. (2022) note that restaurant managers who communicate clearly and attentively with their staff create a positive work atmosphere. This approach can help mitigate some challenges that may arise during stressful periods.

Strategies for Enhancing Employee Engagement

Employee engagement is critical to restaurant success, influencing productivity, customer satisfaction, and overall organizational performance (Bakker & Albrecht, 2018). Unlike simple employee retention, which focuses on keeping employees within the organization, engagement involves creating an environment where employees are emotionally and intellectually committed to their work (Bakker & Albrecht, 2018). Engaged employees are more likely to go above and beyond in their roles, leading to better service quality and customer experiences, which are vital in the hospitality industry.

Training and Development

Training and development are crucial in enhancing employee engagement within an organization. Companies can demonstrate their commitment to fostering their workforce's professional growth and skill development by regularly organizing training sessions (Bilderback, 2024). Research conducted by Al-Kassem (2021) shows that employees who see opportunities for promotion are significantly more likely to exhibit higher levels of commitment and dedication to their roles. This finding is significant in the restaurant industry, which is known for its fast-paced and ever-evolving nature.

Staying current with the latest trends, culinary techniques, and customer service practices is essential for success in this sector. Regular training equips employees with the necessary skills and fosters a sense of belonging and loyalty to the organization, ultimately leading to improved performance and customer satisfaction (Rane et al., 2023). By investing in their employees' development, restaurants can cultivate a more engaged and motivated workforce, vital for thriving in a competitive market.

Providing Flexible Work Schedules

Implementing flexible work arrangements is a strategic approach that can significantly enhance employee engagement and satisfaction. According to Bella (2023), organizations can create a healthier work-life balance by allowing employees to tailor their work hours to better suit their personal lives. This flexibility helps reduce stress levels and plays a critical role in preventing burnout, particularly in high-pressure environments (Uka & Prendi, 2021).

Flexible scheduling becomes even more essential in industries like restaurants, where shifts can be unpredictable and often involve long hours (Kamalahmadi & Zhou, 2021).

Allowing staff to choose shifts that suit their availability can improve morale and productivity, as employees are more likely to be engaged when they feel their needs are considered (Piso, 2022).

Ababneh (2021) emphasized that fostering a culture of participative management can significantly enhance employee engagement. Employees who believe their opinions and suggestions are valued tend to feel a stronger connection to the organization's goals and objectives (Yandi et al., 2022). This sense of ownership encourages them to actively participate in team initiatives and problem-solving efforts (Frega, 2021).

Regular feedback sessions and team meetings are crucial to cultivating this environment. Feedback sessions allow employees to voice their ideas and concerns, making them feel involved in decision-making (Azevedo et al., 2021). When employees see that their contributions are acknowledged and appreciated, they cultivate a more profound sense of belonging and commitment to their work and the organization as a whole(Byrd, 2022).

Including Employees' Input in Decision Making

Restaurant managers should prioritize integrating employee feedback during training and development programs to build a more committed and effective team. (Ogundipe et al., 2024). Engaging employees in these initial stages sets a strong foundation for their organizational commitment, which should be reinforced by fostering a positive organizational culture that encourages open communication and collaboration (Tyagi, 2021). A supportive work environment where employees feel valued and heard naturally increases motivation and commitment.

Flexible work arrangements also play a crucial role in this process. Leaders can improve job satisfaction and enhance overall productivity by allowing employees to tailor their schedules and work environments to better suit their personal needs (Nassani et al., 2024). Actively involving employees in the decision-making process is essential. This can be achieved through regular feedback sessions, surveys, and collaborative meetings, where employees can share their insights and suggestions. When employees see that their opinions matter and can influence the organization's direction, their sense of ownership and loyalty grows (Rampen et al., 2023). Restaurant managers can enhance employee happiness and drive excellent business results by implementing a comprehensive strategy. This includes involving staff in training, fostering a positive culture, providing flexible scheduling, and engaging them in decision-making.

(Dalkhjav et al., 2024).

Designing and Implementing Career Development Opportunities

Companies that provide career enhancement and promotion opportunities have a powerful tool to improve the workforce's loyalty (Urme, 2023). In the same perspective, Ghani et al. (2022) posited that providing career advancement initiatives is one of the effective ways to promote high levels of employee retention in the hospitality industry. Offering skill enhancement and training helps to improve the talents of the employees and the organizations since it leads to a sense of loyalty. Niati et al. (2021) argued that organizations that take time to train and develop their human capital will have better chances of retaining their talented employees.

Restaurant owners should identify key reasons for high employee turnover rates by offering employee satisfaction surveys and feedback on career advancements (Ghani, 2022). It is crucial to design efficient strategies to address the relationship between career development and employee retention. Restaurant owners should apply the best career management practices, like training and career progression, to increase employee retention (Ghani et al., 2021).

Providing career development opportunities enables employees to gain new skills and proves that the organization values their development (Dachner et al., 2021). In this respect, such an investment can return improved job satisfaction, motivation, and even increased commitment to an organization. Where a clear career path for progression is visible to an employee within a current employment situation, they are more likely to remain employed than look for work elsewhere (George & George, 2022). In conclusion, adequate design and implementation of career development opportunities enhance employee management in the restaurant industry. With a clear understanding of their career aspirations, relevant training and development programs provided by restaurant owners can catalyze a more committed and satisfied workforce (Susanto et al., 2023).

Building a Positive Work Environment

According to Ghani et al. (2022), building and promoting a positive work environment is a key strategy for employee retention that restaurant owners can implement in their management practices. Employee retention requires providing an organization with a quality work environment. While losing some employees is unavoidable, designing a retention strategy for promoting a positive work environment can substantially mitigate turnover costs and time lost from recruiting and training new employees (Surangi & Dissanayake, 2021).

Sepahvand and Bagherzadeh Khodashahri (2021) opined that retaining employees helps organizations guarantee the commitment of talented employees so that they may not leave to work for other organizations. Experienced employees are invaluable, and their absence can cause financial and operational problems for the organization. According to Enamala and Reddy (2022), when people are supported and feel good about themselves and their colleagues at work, they will find reasons not to quit their jobs, promoting retention.

Establishing an accommodating and pleasant atmosphere motivates employees to stay longer. The more the employees work, the more loyalty and experience they will have in the business, increasing the establishment's productivity and goal achievement (Ghani et al., 2022). Restaurant owners can adopt strategies to foster a welcoming environment, such as implementing employee development programs, recognizing exemplary performance, and encouraging teamwork. (Wang & Wang, 2024).

Job satisfaction and work-life balance can also improve the positive work environment. In this regard, Basem et al. (2022) recommend that restaurant owners intentionally actively implement managerial themes like satisfaction with the job and work-life balance to foster a positive culture for retaining employees. Some specific job satisfaction practices include acknowledging and promoting employees' achievements, providing choice work hours, and ensuring that communication between the management and the workforce is clear and unhampered (Baptiste et al., 2024). Improving the positive factors in the workplace enables restaurant owners to keep their best workers and to increase organizational effectiveness (Gordon & Parikh, 2021). Valued and supported employees will be motivated to remain committed to their positions, resulting in reduced turnover rates and a stable employee pool (Urme, 2023).

Promote Work-Life Balance

Restaurant owners must invest in creating workspaces that provide employees with stimulating and inspiring work culture and a healthy work-life balance. According to Panda and Sahoo (2021), an excellent work-life balance motivates employees and keeps them committed to their organizational jobs, facilitating retention. Managing family and work obligations can be tiring and may bring much stress to the employees depending on the organization's flexibility in work arrangements. According to Faustina et al. (2024), online service delivery programs can improve the work-life balance. Online service delivery programs enable employees to manage their work from home, allowing them to stay with their families and fostering their commitment and loyalty to the organization. Restaurants with such programs are more likely to retain employees by helping them avoid work-related burnout (Chen & Qi., 2022).

Employee retention significantly impacts operational issues and customer service, ultimately affecting profits. Low employee retention can lead to service disruptions, inconsistency in quality, and reduced customer loyalty (Xu et al., 2022). In contrast, stable employees with strong motivation work towards providing excellent service, building strong client relationships, and enhancing the restaurant's reputation. Investing in employee retention strategies allows restaurant managers to improve internal processes and obtain direct rewards in tangible profits. In summary, promoting work-life balance through flexible work arrangements and online service delivery programs is crucial for retaining employees in the restaurant industry. By addressing the work-life balance needs of their employees, restaurant owners can enhance job satisfaction, reduce turnover rates, and improve overall organizational performance (Naig &

Borbon, 2021).

Implement Talent Management

Talented employees tend to be more comfortable with employers supporting their talent development. This makes talent development and management a potential area of organizational investment to retain employees. Kumar (2022) explored the multi-faceted routes of talent management and its influence on tenure and retention concerns. Kumar outlined different paths to retain and avoid employees. For instance, Kumar discussed methods like training and promotion as a means for organizations to support employees' professional development and increase retention rates. According to Bonneton et al. (2022, p. 210), employees are considered "career capitalists" who focus on their career development based on the knowledge capital areas like "knowing-why," "knowing-how," and "knowing-whom". A successful reinforcement of knowledge about these areas increases employee satisfaction and retention. By offering workers opportunities to improve their qualifications and progress in their jobs, employees' job satisfaction is raised, and the employees become committed to their work (Riyanto & Herlisha,

2021).

Support Workers' Well-Being

Restaurant management must implement adequate support for worker well-being. The support can come in various ways. Uba et al. (2023) found employee support a viable retention strategy that works well in the restaurant industry. Uba et al. (2023) revealed that a combination of strategies for the culture of financial support and career growth programs is required. For instance, by paying premiums to staff, using effective methods for setting pay, and providing a well-established comprehensive training program, restaurants can create a compelling value proposition that results in high job satisfaction and staff advancement. This comprehensive solution recognizes workers' diverse needs and expectations of living while dealing with factors like money stability, career advancement, and talent cultivation.

Gordon and Parikh (2021), in their systematic review of the Book, highlighted how managerial actions in independent restaurants benefit employee well-being. Some such strategies were flexible working hours, employee problems being kept confidential, management decisions being transparent, and the management encouraging employees to give their opinions frequently. These are critical practices that are useful in developing a culture of workplace diversity, which in turn aids in regulating work-life interaction, building organizational trust, and increasing organizational commitment and growth (Gordon & Parikh, 2021). These managerial behaviors are incorporated under the perceived organizational support (POS) and perceived supervisor support (PSS), which benefit employees' job performance, reduce turnover rates, and promote organizational well-being. The same authors' review affirmed that these independent restaurants could adopt these strategies effectively despite their constraints, affording them a competitive advantage in the high-turnover hospitality business.

Employees are human beings, just like everyone, who undergo many life challenges that may not appeal to the public. For instance, this may trigger them to share with the management for assistance. Keeping such circumstances confidential is one thing that most employees value within an organization. Transparency between management and employees enhances trust and builds cohesion, enabling employee engagement (Zanabazar et al., 2023). The success of retention strategies depends on how they are integrated, and address the peculiar nature and traits of the food business for the best results (Badmus et al., 2024).

Implementing Effective Leadership and Competitive Organizational Strategies

Effective leadership is essential to developing and implementing effective strategies that enable the restaurant sector to retain employees. This involves a dual focus on serving the business purpose and retaining employees. In the context of the current analysis of the restaurant industry, this would imply that leaders have to form strategies that serve the business purpose, not forgetting that it is essential to retain employees.

The following practices can, however, retain employees; leaders may benefit from communication regarding their strategies. This includes designing and discussing organizational objectives that embrace short- and long-term goals, which help give the employees direction on what to do. Also, engaging employees during the formulation of the strategies is more likely to ensure commitment toward the company's vision, which can help enhance their motivation and improve employee retention.

According to Herzberg (1959), efforts to improve working conditions gradually, provide opportunities for professional growth, and recognize employees' achievements are most effective in increasing employee retention. Hygiene factors include elements of compensation structure and safety, and nourishing the motivational factors that include a fair compensation structure and safety, career opportunities, and recognition motivate the employee (Herzberg et al., 1959). Restaurant owners should aim to improve hygiene and motivational factors simultaneously (Fuster, 2021).

The development of strategies may benefit from an analysis of the restaurant business's employees' existing needs and demands. Managers should be able to work according to certain principles to be flexible and switch to new approaches and ideas in case of inefficiency or employee dissatisfaction (Kalogiannidis et al., 2021). In this way managers can achieve a competitive advantage while guaranteeing that organizational staff are dedicated to the corporation.

Ultimately, the recommendation for restaurant leadership is to develop and execute strategies that align with the market and address factors influencing employee retention (Ghani et al., 2022). By leveraging the concepts of hygiene factors and motivators, leaders can create a work environment that elevates job satisfaction standards, for retaining employees by fostering a positive, thriving organizational culture.

Comparing and Contrasting Previous Research on Employee Retention

Smith et al. (2022) explored qualitative research in the hospitality industry, and concluded that financial motivators and career advancement opportunities highly influence employee retention. This finding aligns with Herzberg's two-factor theory, which emphasizes the importance of hygiene factors and motivators in job satisfaction. Similarly, Kumar (2022) found that implementing talent management practices, such as training, can reduce turnover by providing career growth and development opportunities. Hence multiple researchers have identified the critical role of financial incentives and professional development in retaining employees.

Anning-Dorson (2021) concluded that work flexibility and openness to communication are essential for building an influential work culture. This perspective shifts the focus from financial and career incentives to organizational culture and communication practices. Enamala and Reddy (2022) also highlighted the importance of fostering a positive workplace environment and providing mutual growth opportunities to mitigate attrition. Enamala and Reddy found that non-financial factors like work environment and communication are equally crucial in employee retention.

Ghani et al. (2022) emphasized the importance of compensation in hiring and retaining employees, particularly in the hospitality sector. The authors 'different geographical context, reinforces the universal importance of financial incentives in employee retention. Gordon and Parikh (2021) identified behaviors and activities of restaurant managers that support staff members, contributing to a stronger sense of support and loyalty. Gordon and Parikh found that the role of managerial behavior impacted employee retention strategies.

Self et al. (2022) focused on peer support and organizational embeddedness, finding that these addressing these factors can reduce turnover intentions among restaurant managers. Self et al. introduced the concept of social support within the workplace as a critical factor in retention. Suraihi et al. (2021) emphasized the significant impact of employee turnover on an organization's expenses, productivity, sustainability, competitiveness, and profitability, highlighting the importance of employee retention in saving time and costs. Uba et al. (2023) identified strong connections between cash bonuses, wage strategies, employee training plans, and employee retention in the context of restaurant company staff retention and incentive strategies. Uba et al. (2023) findings collectively suggested that a multifaceted approach addressing financial and non-financial factors is necessary for effective employee retention.

Molotsi et al. (2023) used Herzberg's theory to develop a conceptual framework to enhance academic staff retention in an open-distance e-learning higher education institution in South Africa. Molotsi et al. highlighted the applicability of Herzberg's theory in different sectors and geographical contexts, suggesting its relevance across various industries. Similarly, using Herzberg's two-factor theory, Ganesh and Liu (2022) examined a model connecting employee job satisfaction to the car industry in Beijing, China. Ganesh and Liu found that the working environment, organizational identity, work engagement, perceived leadership style, and fringe benefits influence job satisfaction, underscoring the need to address these strategies.

In summary, multiple studies' findings across different geographical areas support the value of a multi-sectorial model of an integrated approach to employee well-being as necessary for retention in various settings. From the analysis of the Book, comprehensive support for workers, including financial security, career advancement, and a healthy workplace culture, is essential for implementing successful retention policies. My proposed research project will utilize these findings to understand the effective strategies restaurant owners in Birmingham, AL use to retain employees, focusing on financial and non-financial factors to provide a holistic approach to employee retention.

Conceptual Framework

Herzberg's two-factor theory, developed by Frederick Herzberg in 1959, served as the conceptual framework for my doctoral study. This theory distinguishes between hygiene factors and motivational factors. According to the two-factor theory, both variables can influence an employee's job satisfaction or dissatisfaction (Herzberg, 1959). Hygiene factors include work conditions, salary, benefits, and interpersonal relationships with supervisors and coworkers (Herzberg, 1959). These factors can create a baseline level of satisfaction but do not necessarily motivate employees.

In contrast, motivational factors can enhance job satisfaction and drive higher performance. Herzberg's two-factor theory aligned with my research goals. It provided insight into employee turnover and highlights how motivational and hygiene factors affect an employee's level of job satisfaction.

Transition

In Section 2, I reviewed professional and academic Book in this section and discussed their applications to the applied business problem. Section 3 includes project ethics, research methods and design, population, sampling and participants, data collection techniques, interview questions, data organization, data analysis, reliability, and validity. Section 3 will also discuss the ethical issues involved in proposed research and methodology and design. Section 4 outlines the analysis results, the conclusion based on the research findings, and practical recommendations for strategies that restaurant owners can implement to retain team members. Section 4 presents the findings related to the contributions to professional practice, the impact on social change, and the proposed actions and recommendations for future research.

Section 3: Research Project Methodology

Section 3 of the project includes critical elements required for the research project methodology. These elements include the project ethics, the nature of the project, and the population, sampling, and participants. Section 3 also includes data collection activities, the interview questions, data organization and analysis techniques, assuring the study's reliability and validity, and the transition and summary.

Project Ethics

My role as the researcher for this qualitative pragmatic inquiry project was to gather relevant data to address the research question of my project. I oversaw all aspects of the data collection process. My data collection methods included conducting semistructured interviews and reviewing public documents to obtain detailed and insightful data. I selected and utilized appropriate approaches and techniques to establish a good connection with participants, as this is crucial for gathering high-quality data to support the analysis of my project. It is essential to recognize that collecting information can be intricate and potentially jeopardizes an entire research project if not executed effectively (Newman et al., 2021).

Based on my experience in management, I decided to explore effective strategies to improve employee retention. Before pursuing my DBA degree, I never delved into the causes of employee turnover, the topic of employee retention, or this research area. I do not have any relationships with participants involved in this project or direct involvement with the participating restaurant owners.

The Belmont Report offers principles and guidelines to address ethical issues in research involving human subjects. Adhering to the principles of respect, beneficence, and justice outlined in the report is a fundamental consideration for qualitative researchers. My role regarding ethics and the Belmont Report protocol was crucial as it was my responsibility to honor participants' autonomy, safeguard their well-being, and ensure their fairness (National Commission for the Protection of Human Subjects of Biomedical and Behavioral Research, 1979). I am committed to upholding ethical standards both in form and in practice. I adhered to ethical standards and followed the Belmont Report protocol.

My method for acquiring informed consent involved providing potential participants with information about the research and their possible involvement. Obtaining informed consent is critical in acknowledging participants' autonomy as a display of respect, and participants' communication between the researcher and participant is essential for obtaining proper informed consent (Tamminen, 2021). Because informed consent is the ethical foundation of the research study protocol, ensuring participant comprehension is crucial (Balagurunathan & Sethuramen, 2024). As such, I ensured their understanding of the provided information, including the interview procedures, voluntary participation, their right to withdraw after giving consent, the risks and benefits associated with the research, and confidentiality. This was done by utilizing the IRB's consent form and reviewing the potential participants' information to improve their understanding of the process. In my project, informed consent was obtained before I scheduled interviews.

The process for participants to withdraw from my research project was for participants to communicate this decision directly by notifying me orally or in writing. They had the right to withdraw at any time via email, text, or phone without the need to provide a reason or be penalized. Researchers must ensure that participants understand all aspects of study participation to guarantee their independence and respect their decision to withdraw without facing any negative consequences (Kraft et al., 2021). Researchers may offer incentives to encourage participation and maintain involvement (Kraft et al., 2021). I offered incentives to my participants, such as gift cards.

As the researcher, I was committed to upholding ethical standards and protecting the individuals participating in my project. This commitment included concealing participant identities as stipulated by the Institutional Review Board (IRB). I used unique codes instead of participants' names to maintain confidentiality. This method protects the identities of individuals, organizations, and locations, which is critical for ethical research (Gerrard, 2021). Furthermore, I securely stored interview transcripts, which will be retained for 5 years by IRB guidelines. This included employing secure storage methods to ensure the confidentiality of participants and any organizations mentioned in this project. After receiving approval from the IRB, I was assigned an IRB number 02-17-25-1055533 to conduct the final qualitative pragmatic inquiry research. Once the study was concluded, I provided participants with a summary of the study.

Nature of the Project

There are three research methods from which to select: qualitative, quantitative, and mixed methods (Baškarada & Koronios, 2018). I used the qualitative method to address my research question. Qualitative research allows for exploring, describing, and understanding contextual phenomena (Levitt, 2021). A qualitative approach suited my project because I explored a phenomenon within a particular context. Utilizing the qualitative methodology enabled me to explore and identify effective strategies to improve restaurant employee retention.

My research design was a pragmatic inquiry that focused on the approaches of individual decision-makers in addressing real-world problems. Dewey (1908) noted the significance of experiential learning as well as problem-solving through the use of a practical lens. While focusing on experiential learning, Braun and Clarke (2006) indicated that qualitative data should be analyzed flexibly by identifying, analyzing, and interpreting patterns or themes within a given data set. Qualitative pragmatic inquiry is utilized in business research to identify and interpret strategies, develop potential best practices, or analyze complex phenomena within a transorganizational context (Zilber & Zanoni, 2022). Researchers employing this design can also better discover themes and issues than other approaches (Thompson et al., 2022). The proposed qualitative pragmatic inquiry would include inductive reasoning and themes.

Population, Sampling, and Participants

The target population and eligibility criteria for participants for this project were restaurant owners located in Birmingham, AL., who have used effective strategies to retain employees. Applying eligibility criteria can help qualitative researchers obtain rich, nuanced, complex, and detailed data meaningfully addressing their research question (Levitt, 2021). I used professional associations and social connections to reach out to participants, as these avenues can help establish a meaningful researcher-participant relationship. I recruited them through professional associations and social networking channels.

To engage with the participants, I shared details about the research project, explained the informed consent process, and guided them in preparing for the interview per the interview protocol (Appendix A). Establishing a solid working relationship is crucial for sustained access to data sources and ensuring participants' comprehension (Leach et al., 2024). After the initial outreach, I met with the participants in person to build rapport and mutual understanding, enhancing legitimacy and leading to richer data.

I utilized purposive sampling and chose six participants from the population. This method involved selecting participants strategically to ensure that the data gathered aligned with the research question. Smaller sample sizes are more effective in thoroughly examining contextual phenomena than larger ones (Hunziker & Blankenagel, 2024). Achieving data saturation ensures that relevant data are collected from all participants and that all themes have been exhausted (Hennink et al., 2017). I reached data saturation by collecting from participants through semistructured interviews and reviewing documents until no new themes emerged.

Data Collection Activities

I gathered relevant data to address the research question as a researcher. I was the data collection instrument in this project, overseeing all research aspects of the data collection process to address the research question. For data collection, I used semistructured interviews and public documents to collect data from participants. This method, commonly employed by qualitative researchers, captures detailed data that aligns with the exploratory nature of the research aim (Jiang et al., 2021). The semistructured interview was not just suitable but invaluable for my project as it allowed me to capture critical data while allowing participants to express their personalities and views. Its informal nature, use of open-ended questions, uninterrupted participant input, and spontaneous follow-up questions make it suitable for qualitative research (Ganesha & Aithal, 2022).

During the semistructured interviews, I used an interview protocol (see Appendix A) to ensure consistency across multiple participants, mitigate bias, and support validity and reliability. Interview protocols are essential for effectively exploring real-world phenomena and maintaining consistency in the data collection process (Roulston & Halpin, 2022). My interview protocol included scripted opening statements, questions, and prompts for probing and closing comments. Appendix A presents the interview protocol.

As part of the interview and the data collection process, I recorded all the interviews to ensure accurate data capture of all participant's responses. Moreover, all participants was informed of the need to review their transcripts and my notes during the follow-up sessions. This checking process allowed the participants to verify and clarify the information shared and ensure data accuracy. A transcript review was employed to ensure the reliability and credibility of the data collected.

Interview Questions

The interview questions encompassed the following:

1. What effective employee retention strategies are used at your restaurant?

2. What strategies are utilized to give job-related feedback to employees?

3. What strategies have successfully motivated the organization's employees?

4. What strategies are aimed at facilitating employee performance within the organization?

5. What challenges have you faced when developing and implementing strategies to retain your employees?

6. How did you overcome the challenges?

7. How do you measure the success of implementing strategies to sustain your employees?

8. What additional information would you like to share about effective strategies for retaining employees in your restaurant?

Data Organization and Analysis Techniques

I kept research logs and used cataloging and labeling systems to keep track of the data collection and analysis. I used detailed research logs throughout the project to track main events, progress, and any decisions made during the data collection and analysis phases. As a part of the research, I kept a research diary to record the progress, important events, and decisions made during the data-gathering and analysis stages. This log recorded the dates of interviews and follow-up sessions and any events that may affect data analysis. It is important to note that all interview data, in the form of notes, transcripts, and other related documents, were systematically arranged and labeled. The participants and data sets were given unique identification numbers for anonymity and identification at a later date if needed. The digital files will be kept in secured folders with correct labeling on the folder to reflect the file's date, participant code, and data format. While analyzing the data, I developed codes to categorize and highlight specific patterns and trends that will be helped using a digital coding tool. Every shift in perception or modification of an existing concept was documented for consistency in the shifting analysis.

Qualitative data analysis involves gathering, examining, understanding, and presenting data (Khoa et al., 2023). I used Word, Excel, and NVivo software to analyze data from interviews and document reviews. Qualitative researchers who conduct rigorous, high-quality studies creatively engage with the data systematically (Ganesha & Aithal, 2022). I consistently compared data during analysis to ensure its reliability and validity.

The qualitative inquiry I conducted is best suited for thematic analysis, a foundational qualitative data analysis method. Thematic analysis involves developing ideas, meaning, and understanding of qualitative data through coding (Campbell et al., 2021). Qualitative researchers use thematic analysis for conceptual and design thinking in their studies and can integrate reflexivity to ensure thoughtfulness and reflection (Campbell et al., 2021). This approach allows for a deeper understanding of the data findings, leading to better insights into strategies used to retain employees.

I analyzed the data systematically and step-by-step, sometimes repeating the process for better understanding. Engaging with and interpreting the data iteratively will result in insights and explanations (Jasim et al., 2021). Initially, I transcribed the audio recordings of the data. Then, I reviewed the transcripts and listened to the audio recordings to familiarize myself with the data. I then created initial codes using a color scheme to classify all the data, refining the coding through an iterative process. Next, I identified themes within the data, reviewed them, provided definitions, and named them. Subsequently, I summarized the main findings, interpreted the results, and produced the report. This systematic and sequential method will enable me to draw descriptive and explanatory conclusions.

I employed reflexivity to concentrate on the main themes and link them with my project's Book and conceptual framework. Reflexivity aids in determining the themes for analysis from a myriad of possibilities that emerge from the data, the researcher's subjectivity, and the theoretical and conceptual frameworks (Ganesha & Aithal, 2022). Continuously practicing reflexivity assures the validity of themes and conclusions. I also ensured that this data and all raw data were securely stored for 5 years.

Reliability and Validity

Reliability

Reliability and dependability are essential to ensuring that research methodologies and data are applied consistently, accurately, and objectively (Vu, 2021). To ensure dependability in this project, the following strategies were undertaken. These include recording every activity conducted carefully, managing the interview process, and performing member checking after gathering data. The purpose of member checking was to present the interpretations of participants' responses to ensure that the findings were consistent with the intended meaning of the questions posed. I provided participants with the textual transcripts of their interviews to facilitate their observation that nothing has been reported out of context as part of my efforts to maintain participants' anonymity.

As highlighted by Levitt et al. (2021), it is crucial to involve participants actively meaning that one should ensure that the participants fully understand what you are asking them and give them the chance to express their views. This involvement enhances credibility and conscience validity, for assuring the reliability and dependability of the project's findings. In this fashion, this research will be systematic with demonstrable audit trails for enabling other scholars or researchers to evaluate or even duplicate the study given that they undertake clear and elaborate documentation of the methods, procedures, and findings used in the research project. These findings indicated that the type of clear and accurate reporting minimizes the possible unreliability of the research findings whilst increasing the dependability of the project.

Validity

Establishing credibility is the cornerstone of my research project's validity. This was achieved through rigorous member checking of data interpretation and review of interview transcripts. Coleman (2022) emphasized that credibility is paramount for instilling confidence in the research findings.

Transferability refers to applying research findings to other contexts and settings and facilitating repeatability (Tuval-Mashiach, 2021). It is essential to assist readers in assessing the accuracy and reliability of the inferences made and the potential extension of results and conclusions beyond the proposed research setting. To facilitate the determination of transferability by readers and future researchers, I provided detailed descriptions of the research context, methodology, and participant characteristics.

To address confirmability, I probed during interviews, conducted follow-up memberchecking interviews, triangulated data from multiple sources, and provided reflective commentary. Confirmability is critical for accurately reflecting participants' lived experiences in the research findings, devoid of researcher bias (Lim, 2024). Additionally, I will maintain a detailed audit trail of the research process, documenting critical decisions and reflections throughout the study.

I ensured data saturation by iteratively collecting data from participants through semistructured interviews and documentation review until no new themes were identified. Data saturation occurs when no more themes can be generated from the data collected (Rahimi, 2024).

Data saturation enhanced my project's findings' credibility, transferability, and confirmability.

Transition and Summary

This research project aimed to explore and identify effective strategies restaurant owners use to retain employees. Section 3 included the research project ethics, nature of the project, population sampling and participants, data collection activities, interview questions, data organization and analysis, and reliability and validity. As such, the research project method and design, which was a qualitative pragmatic inquiry, are further explained. This included understanding ethical standards, the Belmont Report requirements, and my role as the project practitioner in collecting data. This also included understanding the procedure if participants wanted to withdraw from participating in the project, securing the data, and concealing the identity of the participants. Section 3 also included the population, sampling procedures, data collection techniques, semistructured interviews, and document reviews, the data collection method, and reliability and validity. Section 3 also included data for tracking and organizational purposes, including research logs and reflective journals, cataloging techniques, and data and thematic analysis. Finally, an explanation was provided on how the reliability and validity of the data will be determined. In Section 4, I will complete this project by presenting findings, discussing business contributions, and providing recommendations for professional practice, implications for social change, suggestions for further research, and drawing a conclusion.

Section 4: Findings and Conclusions

Presentation of the Findings

The purpose of this qualitative pragmatic inquiry was to identify and explore

successful strategies restaurant owners use in Birmingham, AL, to improve

employee retention. The presentation of the findings centered around the following

research question: What effective strategies do restaurant owners in Birmingham,

AL., use to retain employees? The findings from this qualitative pragmatic inquiry

revealed four main themes: (a) compensation, (b) acknowledgment and rewards, (c)

management practices, and (d) a positive working environment. Project participants

were invited to participate in the interviews via invitation, and upon acceptance,

they responded to six open-ended interview questions outlined in the interview

protocol (see Appendix). Table 1 provides a summary of the participant population

involved in this project.

Table 1

Participants' Population Summary

Participant	Employment Title	Years of Service	Average Employee Tenure
P1	Owner/Manager	8	6 years
P2	Owner	12	5 years
P3	Owner	6	4.5 years
P4	Owner/Manager	5	3 years
P5	Owner/CEO	18	6.5 years
P6	Owner/Manager/Head Chef	6	2 years

• P1 is a restaurant owner and manager with over 8 years of experience.

They consistently manage a team of 15 to 20 employees with an average

tenure of 6 years and serve an average of 55 to 60 customers daily.

- P2 has 12 years of experience as a restaurant owner and manages two shifts, overseeing 16 employees (eight per shift), with an average tenure of 5 years. This restaurant is located in a high-traffic area and serves an average of 200 to 225 customers daily.

- P3 is a small restaurant owner who has been in business for 6 years. They manage a team of five employees with an average tenure of 4.5 years and serve an average of 25 to 30 customers daily.

- P4 has owned and managed a unique restaurant for 6 years. They supervise a staff of
14, with an average tenure of 3 years, and serve approximately 90 customers daily.

- P5 has 18 years of experience as a CEO and owner of a restaurant and a food truck. P5 manages employees with an average tenure of 6.5 years at the storefront and the food truck, along with various shift managers. The food truck serves approximately
150 customers daily, while the storefront serves about 80 to 85 customers.

- P6 has been the owner, manager, and head chef for 5 years. They manage 19 employees with an average tenure of 2 years and serve 100 to 125 customers daily. Additionally, P6's restaurant handles significant catering events, such as weddings and banquets, averaging around 200 events annually.

Following the interviews, I utilized methodological triangulation to compare data from the semistructured interviews with insights gathered from analyzing organizational documents and artifacts. To ensure the accuracy of the recorded responses, I reached out to each participant for member-checking by sharing my interpretations of their interview transcripts and asking for their confirmation. I also collected publicly available information from corporate chain websites and individual restaurant sites, including details on the types of establishments and the number of restaurants in Birmingham, AL. I transcribed the interviews and methodically analyzed the responses, organizing the information in Microsoft Word while highlighting key points related to three central themes. The transcripts were subsequently uploaded to NVivo for further analysis and data coding. This process revealed four key themes: compensation, acknowledgment and rewards, management practices, and a positive working environment (see Table 2). These themes emerged as the most commonly discussed elements of effective employee retention strategies. **Table 2**

Themes

Theme	Definition	Participants
Compensation	Compensation is the earnings employees receive in return for their contributions to an organization.	P1, P3, P4, P5, P6
Acknowledgment and Rewards	Acknowledgment and rewards are how employers show employee appreciation based on performance.	P1, P2, P3, P5, P6
Management Practices	Managerial practices are the methods and systems managers use to operate an organization effectively.	P1, P2, P4, P5, P6
A Positive Working Environment	A positive workplace is where employees feel valued and recognized for their hard work.	P2, P3, P4, P5, P6

Theme 1: Compensation

Compensation emerged as the first key theme in the data collected from the interviews. Many interviewees underscored that providing fair compensation is an effective tactic for reducing employee turnover and a fundamental aspect of fostering a positive workplace culture. This strategy aligns with the findings of

Werner and Balkin (2021), who emphasized that competitive salaries, comprehensive retirement, and health benefits play a critical role in lowering employee turnover rates. Offering fair wages is crucial for creating job satisfaction and minimizing turnover.

In the heart of a bustling neighborhood, restaurant owner and manager P1 sat down to reflect on the integral role of compensation within their business. As they observed the restaurant's natural rhythm or cycle of activity, it became clear that salary was more than just a number; it was a foundational component of employee engagement and satisfaction. P1 understood small businesses' unique challenges, explaining, "Since we are considered a smaller business, we aim to offer competitive pay that is fair to our employees and sustainable for the business." They knew that to attract and retain talent, they needed to balance what was practical for the company and what was motivating for their team. While P1 recognized that their salary was not the highest in the industry, they felt pride in knowing it was better than most alternatives available to their employees. This commitment to fair compensation was not merely a strategy but a testament to their dedication to fostering a supportive work environment where every team member felt valued. With a deep sense of responsibility, P1 continued to shape its business ethos, believing that when employees are adequately compensated, their engagement flourishes, leading to a vibrant and productive workplace.

This perspective reveals that P1 recognizes the need to evaluate compensation based on experience, education, and work schedules despite being a smaller entity. Additionally, P1's approach includes providing paid time off (PTO) at the beginning of each year. However, they stipulate that additional time off would result in deductions from the employee's income once that PTO is exhausted. This illustrates a balanced approach between employee benefits and business sustainability.

The insights from P1 underscore that compensation, including salary and benefits like paid time off, is essential to overall employee satisfaction. Supporting Book suggests that to remain competitive in the labor market, small business owners can enhance workforce retention and attract qualified candidates by providing benefits such as paid leave (Gabriel & Veronis, 2023). Research indicates that paid time off, which encompasses sick leave, vacation pay, and holiday leave, is significantly linked to higher employee retention rates (Hofmarcher, 2021; Sainju & Hartwell, 2021).

P3 emphasized the crucial role of healthcare benefits within the employee compensation framework. They pointed out that workers who frequently take time off due to health issues tend to demonstrate lower productivity, a finding that is consistent with research by Henderson and Smith (2022). This observation highlights a growing trend among small business owners who are beginning to understand the importance of prioritizing employee health. By providing sufficient healthcare benefits, businesses can improve employee well-being and productivity (Lovejoy et al., 2021). This perspective aligns with the understanding that a healthy workforce is essential for achieving organizational goals.

P4 shared valuable insights regarding retirement plans and their significance for small businesses. They pointed out that many small business owners recognize the importance of offering retirement plans as part of their benefits packages. This thoughtful inclusion allows employees to invest a portion of their paycheck into mutual funds, allowing their savings to grow tax-free until they reach a certain age. It is a win-win situation that supports employees' financial well-being and helps business owners attract and retain top talent in an increasingly competitive job market. P4's perspective highlighted how these retirement options can empower employees to secure their future while fostering a sense of loyalty and commitment to the company.

P4 elaborated that employers often match contributions to these investment plans, although they acknowledged that IRS regulations can pose challenges for small business owners (Hoffman et al., 2021). This dual contribution approach from both employers and employees enhances the financial security of workers, making them feel valued and supported in their longterm financial planning (Pan et al., 2024).

P5 engaged in a spirited discussion about the intricacies of employee compensation, during which one voice emerged with a critical perspective on the relationship between job security and healthcare benefits. This individual emphasized, "It's only fair to offer employees healthcare benefits, especially if they are contributing to your business's goals," a sentiment that resonated deeply. The dialogue revealed that offering robust healthcare benefits is not just a moral obligation but a strategic move to enhance loyalty and commitment within the workforce. This conversation underscored the belief that a supportive workplace is one where employees feel valued and secure, ultimately propelling the company toward shared success. This statement underscores a growing recognition among employers that financial and job security provided by comprehensive health insurance can significantly influence employee loyalty and commitment to the organization. P6 seized the opportunity to share their perspective, explaining how the process works within the organization. "We understand that when employees join us, they agree to the offered compensation," P6 began, capturing everyone's attention. "However, we do allow for negotiations when it comes to determining salary. The important thing to remember is that any reasoning for a request must truly make sense." Leaning slightly, they emphasized: "If an employee can convincingly articulate why they deserve an increased salary, I will consider it. It's all about the rationale behind the request." Their approach highlighted a fundamental belief in open communication and fairness, encouraging employees to advocate for themselves while recognizing the importance of justifiable reasoning in salary discussions. The team nodded in agreement, appreciating P6's balanced view on an often tricky subject. This flexible approach signals a willingness to engage with employees on financial matters, reinforcing a sense of partnership and respect within the employer-employee relationship.

Correlations to Book

In alignment with the findings from Lovejoy et al. (2021), it becomes clear that offering fair wages is fundamental to both retaining existing employees and attracting new talent. The overall analysis indicates that a strategy focused on providing fair compensation is vital for minimizing employee turnover, resonating with Herzberg's two-factor theory, which asserts that salary is a key hygiene factor that significantly influences job dissatisfaction (Herzberg, 1959). Thus, creating a well-rounded compensation strategy is essential for employee retention and building a thriving organizational culture.

Theme 2: Acknowledgement and Rewards

The second theme that emerged from the data is acknowledgment and rewards. Most participants indicated that this strategy is crucial for improving employee retention. Their strategies align with Uba et al. (2023), who noted strong connections between cash bonuses, wage strategies, employee training plans, and staff retention in the context of restaurant companies.

P1 highlighted several key practices to foster a positive and motivating work environment. They shared that employees are awarded raises and bonuses based on their performance and receive paid days off as a tangible way of showing appreciation for their hard work. This approach reflects a commitment to valuing each individual's contribution to the team. In addition to financial incentives, P1 emphasized the power of verbal recognition. They believe proactively encouraging employees and acknowledging their accomplishments can significantly impact morale and productivity. P1 remarked, "I always remind my employees that we cannot operate without them. They are the reason we are still here. I cannot do this alone." This statement underlines P1's belief in the team's collective effort and their understanding that success is a shared achievement. By fostering an environment where employees feel valued and recognized, P1 aims to cultivate loyalty and motivation.

P1's response is consistent with Koncar et al. (2022), who posited that rewards lead to employee engagement, which drives motivation and enhances job satisfaction. According to the two-factor theory (Herzberg, 1959), rewards and recognition are essential motivational factors that can increase job satisfaction and reduce employee turnover.

In the heart of a bustling city, where the streets were always alive with the hum of activity, P2 thrived in this fast-paced environment, understanding that behind the restaurant's success lay a crucial element: the well-being of his staff. P2 believed recognition was a powerful motivator that significantly enhanced job satisfaction, often reflecting on workplace dynamics and how easy it was for people to focus on mistakes rather than achievements. With a thoughtful demeanor, he addressed this challenge head-on, noting, "Everyone is always quick to point out what went wrong instead of what is going right." P2 consistently awarded good work to counteract this tendency, celebrating even minor victories, from a perfectly executed dish to a well-managed busy shift. His recognition didn't go unnoticed; employees felt appreciated and valued, encouraging them to go above and beyond.

P2 observed that the more he acknowledged their hard work, the more they embraced his philosophy of excellence, reinforcing the concepts defined by the two-factor theory and illustrating how intrinsic motivation could drive success in the workplace. As stories of the restaurant's vibrant atmosphere and outstanding service spread, P2's commitment to his employees and customers transformed his establishment into a beloved local gem, thriving not just on the foundation of great food but also on the strong bonds formed within the team, all thanks to P2's dedication to fostering a positive work environment. P3 added the following:

If you have a great staff, why not reward them? I find every opportunity to reward my staff; for example, we celebrate birthdays. Whenever one of my staff's birthdays comes around, we meet as a team and enjoy cake and ice cream. I also host a yearly holiday party where employees can invite two guests. We have a live band, games, giveaways, and dinner. These are extra incentives I offer to show appreciation. When people feel appreciated, it creates a healthy morale.

Acknowledging and rewarding employees for their hard work and achievements can boost morale and job satisfaction. Implementing programs recognizing employee contributions, such as 'Employee of the Month' awards or performance bonuses, fosters appreciation and loyalty (Koncar et al., 2022). Organizations should prioritize employee recognition, enhancing engagement, and contributing to a more productive work culture.

P5 believed that in the restaurant atmosphere, decision-making lay in the team's collective wisdom. Committed to fostering inclusivity, I organized bi-weekly meetings, eagerly opening the floor to feedback and suggestions from employees. During these gatherings, P5 was genuinely interested in shared perspectives, often stating, "My employees often have great ideas," emphasizing the synergy that emerged from collaboration. This simple yet powerful philosophy that more pairs of eyes are better than one empowered the team and led to innovative solutions that benefited everyone. P5 cherished these moments of open dialogue, knowing they could achieve more together than any individual could alone. They could achieve more than any individual could alone.

Feedback from various sources, coworkers, managers, supervisors, and customers, is essential for employee recognition (Bregenzer et al., 2022). When a job fosters personal development or provides a sense of purpose, it can lead to feelings of achievement and fulfillment. Meaningful, high-quality work contributes to growth and accomplishment (Wahyudi,

2022). P6 explained how employee engagement drives motivation. P6 noted

> I see the excitement in my employees when they feel included and engaged. Whenever I agree with suggestions, I challenge them to create a game plan for how we will proceed. This approach empowers the team and cultivates a sense of shared purpose and accountability.

Employee engagement can enhance motivation and job satisfaction. Koncar et al. (2022) affirmed that rewards can lead to employee engagement. When employees are recognized for their work, they develop a bond with the company and are more likely to remain in their positions. According to Herzberg (1959), recognition is a motivating factor that results in job satisfaction and can lead to enhanced employee retention.

Theme 3: Management Practices

The third theme addresses management practices, which participants indicated as a strategy to enhance employee retention. This aligns with Herzberg's (1959) two-factor theory, which posits that supervision is a hygiene factor that can lead to job dissatisfaction. P1 emphasized that effective management hinges on good communication. Transparent and open communication between management and employees fosters trust and helps address concerns before they escalate.

Regular feedback sessions, team meetings, and an open-door policy make employees feel valued and heard (Gordon & Parikh, 2021). By incorporating these strategies, restaurant owners can cultivate a work environment that meets employee needs and expectations, subsequently improving retention rates and workforce motivation and satisfaction.

P2 highlighted the importance of trustworthiness and honesty in management for earning respect. According to Ndlovu et al. (2021), fostering open and honest communication significantly enhances employee commitment and job satisfaction. However, some leaders may struggle with maintaining consistent recognition and communication practices, potentially undermining the effectiveness of these strategies (Franzosa et al., 2022). Mistry et al. (2022) noted that restaurant managers who communicate clearly with their staff create a positive work atmosphere, which can help mitigate challenges during stressful periods. P4 stated the following: A good manager is present and follows the rules and protocols. Employees question how they could trust a manager who is rarely present or does not practice what they preach. P4 described their management style as hands-on, emphasizing the importance of being involved with the team to better understand and address any issues that arise.

Inadequate supervision can lead to job dissatisfaction and increased employee turnover. Kalogiannidis et al. (2021) confirmed that poor supervision and stress contribute to turnover intentions, reinforcing Herzberg's two-factor theory. Therefore, supervisors must know their employees' workloads to prevent burnout. P5 noted that

Ensuring adequate staff availability helps prevent employees from feeling overwhelmed.

Checking in with employees and offering assistance fosters a supportive environment.

P6 discussed the importance of adaptability in management, stating that

Managers must know their team and what strategies work best for each

individual. By doing so, managers can achieve a competitive advantage while

ensuring their staff remains dedicated to the organization.

P6's response aligns with the second component of my study, which focuses

on transformational leadership theory. Eaton (2024) found that employees are

likelier to follow leaders who demonstrate confidence, passion, and the ability to

inspire others to achieve common goals. Effective management necessitates

flexibility and a willingness to adopt new approaches to address inefficiencies or

employee dissatisfaction (Kalogiannidis et al., 2021).

Successful management practices are crucial for developing and

implementing strategies that help retain employees in the restaurant sector. This

requires a dual focus on meeting business objectives while preserving employee

satisfaction. Adopting an appropriate leadership style, such as transformational

leadership, is essential for organizational success (Lasrado & Kassem, 2021).

Leaders should communicate their strategies clearly and involve employees in

formulating organizational objectives that include both short- and long-term goals.

This collaborative approach enhances motivation and commitment to the company's

vision.

Herzberg (1959) suggested that gradually improving working conditions, offering opportunities for professional growth, and recognizing employee achievements are crucial for increasing retention. Hygiene factors, such as compensation and safety, must be addressed alongside motivational factors, like fair pay and career opportunities (Herzberg et al., 1959). Restaurant owners should strive to concurrently enhance hygiene and motivational factors (Fuster, 2021).

Ultimately, the recommendation is to prioritize management practices that foster communication, trust, and adaptability to improve employee retention within the restaurant industry. Effective management practices are essential to developing and implementing effective strategies that enable the restaurant sector to retain employees. This involves a dual focus on serving the business purpose and retaining employees. In the context of the current analysis of the restaurant industry, this would imply that leaders have to form strategies that serve the business purpose, not forgetting that it is essential to retain employees.

Leaders may benefit from communicating their strategies, including designing and discussing organizational objectives that embrace short- and long-term goals. This approach helps give employees clear direction on what to do. Additionally, engaging employees during the formulation of these strategies is more likely to ensure their commitment to the company's vision, which can enhance motivation and improve employee retention.

According to Herzberg (1959), efforts to improve working conditions gradually, provide opportunities for professional growth, and recognize employees' achievements are most effective in increasing employee retention. Hygiene factors

include elements of compensation structure and safety, and nourishing the motivational factors that include a fair compensation structure and safety, career opportunities, and recognition motivate the Employee (Herzberg et al., 1959). Restaurant owners should simultaneously aim to improve hygiene and motivational factors
(Fuster, 2021).

Ultimately, restaurant leadership should develop and execute strategies that align with the market and address factors influencing employee retention (Ghani et al., 2022). By leveraging the concepts of hygiene factors and motivators, leaders can create a work environment that elevates job satisfaction standards and fosters a positive, thriving organizational culture, which can help retain employees.

Theme 4: A Positive Work Environment

The data exploration led to a critical theme of fostering a positive work environment. Participants unanimously articulated that creating a caring and clean work atmosphere is a fundamental strategy for reducing employee turnover. This can be achieved through flexible work hours, mental health support programs, and recognition of personal milestones. Their insights underscore the importance of demonstrating genuine concern for employees, not only as workers but as individuals with lives and obligations outside their jobs.

P1 articulated this sentiment succinctly:

It is all about showing empathy. My employees are humans first. They have responsibilities outside of work. I understand that kids get sick, that as parents grow older, they face health issues, and that I recognize the need for mental health days.

This perspective resonates with the findings of Uka and Prendi (2021), which emphasize that employees who can strike a balance between their professional and personal lives are more likely to remain loyal to their employers. The data suggests that businesses with programs and policies that promote work-life balance see lower turnover rates, indicating that a supportive culture is crucial for employee retention.

P2 emphasized the importance of trust in the workplace, articulating that a truly positive work environment is characterized by employees who feel secure and confident in their management. P2 elaborated that when employees perceive an atmosphere of openness and reliability, it fosters collaboration and enhances overall productivity. Trust encourages individuals to voice their ideas and concerns without fear, leading to a more engaged and motivated workforce. In essence, a workplace grounded in trust nurtures employee well-being and drives organizational success.

This assertion aligns with a fundamental aspect of organizational behavior, and trust is a cornerstone of effective management. Managers' ability to keep their promises, treat all employees equitably, and maintain confidentiality is paramount. P2's insights align with research by Gordon and Parikh (2021), which indicates that small business owners who foster trust through interpersonal relationships and maintain transparent communication can significantly reduce voluntary turnover. This underscores the clear relationship between trust and retention, reassuring the audience that their trust-building efforts can yield positive results.

P3 brought a valuable perspective to the discussion by positing that empowering employees to voice their ideas increases engagement and loyalty. P3 shared how their organization welcomes suggestions for improving operational aspects, such as building maintenance. This practice shows that management values employee contributions and enhances workplace culture. P3 concurred with Rampen et al. (2023), who found that employees are likelier to display loyalty and feel a sense of ownership when they know their input is respected and can impact the organization's trajectory. Involving employees in decision-making processes cultivates creativity, teamwork, and job satisfaction, as articulated by Basalamah and As'ad

(2021).

The sentiments expressed by the participants collectively highlight that when employees feel genuinely valued, they are less inclined to leave their positions. Several interviewees identified management's understanding and support as motivating factors for their organizational commitment. Enamala and Reddy (2022) corroborated this idea, stating that strong supervisor support can reduce employees' intentions to leave their roles. When employees perceive appreciation and backing from their leaders, they often find compelling reasons to remain with the organization. Furthermore, flexible work arrangements emerged as a demonstration of concern for employee well-being. Managers are encouraged to maintain flexibility and adaptability in response to inefficiencies or signs of employee dissatisfaction (Kalogiannidis et al., 2021).

P4 shared a noteworthy example:

> People who work for me have kids, a spouse, etc. I accommodate their schedule as much as possible. This primarily benefits those wanting to participate in field trips with their kids or school programs. By allowing them

to adjust their hours or take time off as needed, I aim to support their family commitments while fostering a positive and productive work environment. P4's approach shows that granting employees autonomy over their schedules enhances job satisfaction and empowers them to balance work and personal commitments effectively. Supporting this view, Ghani et al. (2022) indicated that leadership behavior is critical in influencing turnover intentions. P5 reinforced the significance of demonstrating care in management practices, remarking,

> Showing you care is crucial in management. My company offers two personal holidays that can be taken whenever needed, as long as they are requested promptly. I am lenient with work schedules, especially for college students whose schedules change each semester. I genuinely care about them, not just their work performance but also their future.

P5's observation highlights a pattern where employees are willing to go above their prescribed roles in appreciation of a supportive management style.

A positive work environment is not just beneficial for employee retention; it significantly enhances job satisfaction. Recognition of individual contributions and achievements, teamwork appreciation, and open communication promotion can significantly enhance employee engagement and morale (Koncar et al., 2022). Acknowledgment is a motivating factor, reinforcing employees' efforts are valued. This should inspire the audience to implement or enhance recognition programs, driving employees to contribute more energetically to their organization.

Creating and promoting supportive and inclusive work environments is not just good practice; it's crucial in bolstering employee morale and overall satisfaction. Such environments are foundational in building robust relationships between staff and management, fostering a safe, healthy atmosphere conducive to productivity, and cultivating a culture rooted in respect and tolerance (Ali & Anwar, 2021). This reiteration should make the audience feel the urgency of creating such an environment in their organizations.

Collectively, the perspectives shared by all interviewees align with Herzberg's two-factor theory, which articulates that working conditions and interpersonal relationships are pivotal in contributing to job satisfaction, ultimately leading to lower employee turnover (Herzberg, 1959). Herzberg's research indicates that enhancing working conditions can significantly improve employee satisfaction, and the consensus from our participants strongly advocates that a caring, clean work environment is essential for minimizing turnover rates.

Business Contributions and Recommendations for Professional Practice

The findings of this pragmatic inquiry are essential for restaurant owners in Birmingham, AL, as they implement strategies to improve employee retention. Restaurant owners can use the study results when formulating leadership strategies to enhance employee retention. The research findings highlighted how compensation, acknowledgment and rewards, management practices, and a positive working environment can be applied to improve employee retention. Uka and Prendi (2021) described that factors such as recognition, achievement, and responsibility are the factors that define motivation and satisfaction at work. These components extend to (a) compensation, the earnings employees receive in return for their contributions to an organization, (b) acknowledgment and rewards are how employers show employee appreciation based on performance,(c) management practices are the methods and systems managers use to operate an organization effectively, and (d) a positive working environment, which is one where employees feel valued and recognized for their hard work.

Implications for Social Change

The findings of this pragmatic study have significant implications for reducing unemployment rates, training restaurant and business owners, increasing the profitability of small businesses, and identifying effective employee retention strategies used by restaurant owners. By implementing the proven strategies, the restaurant owners will be able to create a more stable and committed workforce. Strengthening the employee retention will lead to tangible benefits such as improved teamwork, morale, and greater financial stability for the employees, in turn leading to enhance customer service. Higher retention rates will also lead to reduced turnover rates, in turn fostering a long-term sustainability of the restaurant industry.

Recommendations for Further Research

Restaurant owners who lack strategies should consider using Herzberg's two-factor theory, which is consistent with my study's findings. They should use the results of this pragmatic inquiry to evaluate their current HR strategies to mitigate employee retention. The study contributes knowledgeably to the actions taken by restaurant operators in Birmingham, AL, towards improving staff turnover. However, various limitations need further consideration in future research. One limitation includes geographic generalizability, which may prevent the study results from being generalized to other regions since it only focused on the restaurant

sector in Birmingham. It is essential to pay attention to the peculiarities of the

economic, cultural, and demographic situation in Birmingham to identify the factors

that may cause changes in the tendencies of employee turnover differently as

opposed to those in other metropolitan or rural areas. The generalization of the

results may be facilitated by expanding the study to different geographical regions.

Thus, analyzing a more significant number of company contexts, the researchers

will identify whether the described tactics are helpful or the specific regional

changes that will support employee retention in the restaurant industry.

Another limitation is the use of gathered data from the proprietors of

restaurants, which may create self-bias or lack of information. It is recommended

that future research use a crosssectional design where interviews should be

conducted alongside employee questionnaires to understand staff retention

strategies better from the firms' and employees' perspectives. The main drawback

of the present work was the restriction of time and, therefore, less comprehensive

coverage of the longitudinal period. Another limitation was that some restaurant

owners may depend on others for management decisions, which could result in a

lack of immediate information and insights. Additionally, participants may have

chosen to withhold crucial details about their business strategies and practices,

especially given the fact that this study primarily interviewed the restaurant owners.

Future studies should employ a longitudinal research design and observe the

retention of employees for long periods to have a more elaborate understanding of compensation, management practices, rewards, and the physical working environment.

Restaurant owners should look into the integration of Herzberg's two-factor theory into current employee engagement models. For that reason, research in the future may investigate the effects of psychological safety climate, the role of emotional intelligence in leaders, and flexibility at work on the retention of the workforce. Also, it will be beneficial to study the direct impact of the transformational leadership theory on aspects suc

h as employee engagement, innovation, and commitment. Managers of the restaurant may increase the retention of workers and reduce turnover with the help of these techniques. The study's implications are helpful for restaurant managers and employers, business leaders and executives, and policy-makers to establish feasible ways of retaining hospitality employees.

Conclusion

In my qualitative pragmatic inquiry study, I aimed to identify and explore effective strategies used by successful restaurant owners in Birmingham, AL, for retaining employees. The study findings affirm the findings of Herzberg's (1959) two-factor theory in employee motivation and hygiene factors' contribution to employee retention. Thus, according to the study's conclusions, the principal antecedents of retention include a favorable work climate, effective practices in the workplace, wages, and recognition and reward. By implementing the proven strategies-(competitive compensation including fair wages, benefits, retirement plans, acknowledgment and Rewards including bonuses, recognition programs, effective Management Practices and a Positive Working Environment including a work-life balance, inclusivity), the restaurant owners will be able to create a more stable and committed workforce. Strengthening the employee retention will lead to tangible benefits such as improved teamwork, morale, and greater financial stability for the employees, in turn leading to enhance customer service. Higher retention rates will also lead to reduced turnover rates, in turn fostering a long-term sustainability of the restaurant industry. Employers may be also able to boost employee loyalty and decrease employee turnover by recognizing and showing appreciation for their employees' hard work and successes. My study showed that there is a need for performance incentives and, more so, recognition of prompts for commitment to work and job satisfaction. Furthermore, an effective restaurant owner understands the role they play in impacting employee retention by building a positive workplace culture so that it becomes a powerful tool for retaining top talent. Trust, open communication, and engagement of the employees in the workplace were highly likely to be promoted in companies where management applied effective management practices and knowledge that aligned most with transformational leadership theory. Finally, a work environment that is rich and encompassing with a primary focus on the workers is the most effective strategy to retain employees, the most valuable assets of any organization, to enhance the restaurant's profitability.

www.ingramcontent.com/pod-product-compliance
Lightning Source LLC
Chambersburg PA
CBHW071513210326
41597CB00018B/2739